Series 117

This is a Ladybird Expert book, one of a series of titles for an adult readership. Written by some of the leading lights and outstanding communicators in their fields and published by one of the most trusted and well-loved names in books, the Ladybird Expert series provides clear, accessible and authoritative introductions, informed by expert opinion, to key subjects drawn from science, history and culture.

The Publisher would like to thank the following for the illustrative references for this book:
Page 25: Corbis via Getty Images; page 31: Keystone / Getty Images;
page 51: Pictorial Press Ltd / Alamy Stock Photo

Every effort has been made to ensure images are correctly attributed; however, if any omission or error has been made, please notify the Publisher for correction in future editions.

PENGUIN MICHAEL JOSEPH

UK | USA | Canada | Ireland | Australia
India | New Zealand | South Africa

Penguin Michael Joseph is part of the Penguin Random House group of companies
whose addresses can be found at global.penguinrandomhouse.com

 Penguin
Random House
UK

First published 2023
001

Text copyright © James Holland, 2023

All images copyright © Ladybird Books Ltd, 2023

The moral right of the author has been asserted

Printed in Italy by L.E.G.O. S.p.A.

The authorized representative in the EEA is Penguin Random House Ireland,
Morrison Chambers, 32 Nassau Street, Dublin D02 YH68

A CIP catalogue record for this book is available from the British Library

ISBN: 978–0–718–18728–6

www.greenpenguin.co.uk

Victory in Europe 1944–1945

James Holland

With illustrations by
Keith Burns

Ladybird Books Ltd, London

Just a couple of weeks after the Allies had landed in Normandy on D-Day, the Soviet Red Army was poised to launch its biggest-ever offensive: Operation BAGRATION, named personally by Stalin, the Soviet leader, after the Russian field marshal mortally wounded at Borodino in 1812. Much of the Soviet Union lands lost to Germany had been retaken but the Baltic states were still in German hands and a huge bulge pressed into Belarus to the north of the giant Pripyet Marshes. BAGRATION aimed to push that giant salient back and smash the German Army Group Centre.

The Red Army had changed greatly since June 1941 when the Germans invaded. It was better trained, better organized and better led. Men like Marshal Constantin Rokossovsky, commanding the First Belorussian Front, were vastly experienced and supremely able. Rokossovsky even had the courage of his convictions to stand up to Stalin over the detailed planning of BAGRATION. Stalin conceded the point and allowed Rokossovsky to launch a two-fisted attack either side of the city of Bobruisk.

Partisans operating behind German lines but in touch with Stavka, the Soviet high command, were ordered to attack railways and other German communication lines. Some 143,000 partisans, organized into brigades and detachments, wreaked havoc. On 20 June alone, 147 trains were derailed.

At the front, the Red Army had amassed 2.4 million men against 1.2 million German troops, but the real difference lay in the arms they could bring to bear: 36,400 guns against 9,500; 5,200 tanks against 900; and 5,300 aircraft against 1,350. Red Army offensives began rather like a giant battering ram being swung into the enemy with immense force. BAGRATION began on 22 June, almost three years to the day from the German invasion of the Soviet Union.

With what little remained of the Luftwaffe busy battling the Allied bomber offensive or grounded through lack of fuel, Red Army Shturmoviks, robust ground-attack aircraft, pulverized German anti-tank guns and forward positions, and the huge concentration of force that followed on the ground was unstoppable. By 28 June, Rokossovsky's troops had destroyed the German Ninth Army, had forced Fourth Army into retreat and badly mauled Third Panzer. Bobruisk fell to the Red Army, then, on 3 July, so did Minsk. By the following day, Army Group Centre had lost a staggering 25 divisions. Such was the depth of Red Army logistics, the Soviet juggernaut rolled on beyond Minsk, something the Germans had not expected. It was what the Soviets called 'deep battle'.

Hitler demanded Vilnius in Lithuania be held to the last man, but it still fell on 13 July. Defying the terrain, the Red Army then used log roads to move 3,500 artillery pieces and over 30,000 vehicles through the Pripyet Marshes, allowing the First Belorussian Front to press on into Poland. Overwhelming force, deep-battle tactics and Hitler's insistence on no retreats destroyed Army Group Centre.

By the end of July, the Red Army had crossed the River Vistula but by then they were running out of steam. The Soviet way of war was very effective but incredibly costly to themselves too. By the time BAGRATION finally came to a halt on 19 August, the Germans had lost 771,000 men and most of their equipment, but the Red Army had lost 757,000 – almost as many – of which 178,507 were killed. These were staggering – and unsustainable – numbers, even for the Soviet Union.

Meanwhile, on 1 August the Warsaw Uprising began. The Polish Resistance aimed to push the Germans back out of the city but also to assert Polish sovereignty ahead of the Soviet advance.

The Warsaw Uprising was to prove one of the terrible tragedies of the war. Initially, the Germans were successfully driven out of the city, but the much-needed Soviet support was not forthcoming. Rather, the Red Army sat back while the Germans exacted swift and savage revenge. British Prime Minister Winston Churchill pleaded in vain with Stalin to allow the RAF to use Red Army airfields. Eventually, 200 supply drops were flown over from Allied bases in Italy, but it was not enough. German reinforcements were brought in under command of SS General Erich von dem Bach. Retribution was brutal with groups of soldiers moving door-to-door and street-to-street slaughtering inhabitants regardless of age or gender.

Short of supplies and with casualties mounting, the Uprising collapsed, although pockets of resistance continued until the end of September. In all, around 15,000 Polish Home Army troops were killed but a further 150,000–200,000 civilians were slaughtered and much of the rest of the civilian population cleared from the city. It was a terrible, merciless episode.

Meanwhile, on the Western Front, the Allies were able to capture huge swathes of land following the German collapse in Normandy. While the Canadian First Army moved up the Channel coast, British Second Army swept over the River Seine and pushed on into Belgium. Brussels was liberated on 3 September amidst cheering crowds, while to the south the US First and Third Armies made giant strides eastwards across most of France. More ground was retaken in fewer days than the Germans had achieved coming from the opposite direction back in May 1940.

France was also being liberated from the south. French and US troops had landed in Provence on 15 August and were now pushing up the Rhone Valley and meeting only weak resistance.

The Germans were pulling back on almost all fronts but Hitler now ordered his V-2 rockets to be launched. These were an astonishing technical achievement and the first man-made object to enter space. These ballistic supersonic missiles carried a warhead of nearly a ton of high explosive and were terrifying weapons for the civilians on the receiving end. The first landed on Paris and London on 8 September, but they were neither accurate enough nor plentiful enough to be remotely decisive. In fact, more slave labourers, many of them Soviet POWs and Jews, died manufacturing them in brutal conditions than were killed as a result of the explosions they caused.

The Luftwaffe also had pioneering new jet aircraft, but Hitler insisted these should be used as bombers rather than defensive fighters, the role for which they had been designed. Again, there were not enough of them to make a difference to the outcome of the war, nor were the engines strong enough to last more than about 20 hours of combat flying.

In contrast, the Allies now had enormous fleets of bombers equipped with ever-improving navigational and targeting aids. The differences between RAF night-time 'area' bombing and US daylight 'precision' bombing were blurring. On 10 September, for example, the US Eighth Air Force sent out 1,145 heavy bombers escorted by 705 fighters to nine different targets. The following night, Bomber Command sent out 226 aircraft to attack synthetic fuel plants at Darmstadt and a further 412 against oil targets during the day on the 12th, and a further 378 bombers on the night of 12/13 September. It was relentless and it was having a devastating effect on both German fuel supplies and cities.

While BAGRATION had been rolling through Belorussia, the Red Army had also launched a thrust through southern Ukraine, smashing the combined German and Romanian opposition, sweeping through Moldavia and prompting King Michael of Romania to mount a successful coup against the Fascist Marshal Antonescu. On 23 August, Romania declared war on Germany, its ally for much of the war, which meant the Nazi regime lost its last source of real oil. On 7 September, Bulgaria, which had allied with Germany through much of the war, also switched sides.

It was no wonder the Allies were hopeful of ending the war by Christmas. The Luftwaffe had retrenched to the Reich and was throwing increasingly poorly trained pilots to the slaughter. Germany's navy had been largely destroyed, while its army was suffering one devastating blow after another and, for the most part, was on the run. Despite the Nazis' possession of vengeance weapons like the V-2, it was strikingly clear the war was lost and almost any other leader than Hitler would have called an end to it. But the Führer was not like other leaders. Ideologically driven, he was determined to continue his annihilation of Europe's Jews and to fight to the bitter end. In Hitler's world view, there would be either a Thousand Year Reich or Armageddon. But there would be no surrender.

By the first week of September, the rapid Allied advances in the west were beginning to slow down as supply lines, running all the way back to Normandy, became overextended, and as the shattered German forces started to regain some order out of the chaos of defeat and retreat. On 7 September, however, a daring plan was agreed to use airborne troops to help win the war in 1944.

Despite the defeats the German Army had suffered, the Allied high command was aware the Germans might well want to fight on bitterly to defend the Reich itself. Much of Germany was bordered by a number of rivers, including the mighty Rhine, and dense forests, as well as the Siegfried Line, or Westwall – deep border defences of bunkers, mines, wire and gun emplacements. In northern Holland, however, the Westwall ended and the Rhine was narrower. If the Allies could break across the Rhine here, the route into Germany might be much easier – and once they had a firm foothold in Germany itself then total enemy collapse might follow and the war be over quickly.

Field Marshal Sir Bernard Montgomery, commander of the Anglo-Canadian 21st Army Group, argued to use the Allied Airborne Army to capture a series of bridges, the last of which, at the Dutch town of Arnhem, crossed the Rhine. While paratroopers and gliders secured and held the bridges, an armoured corps would go hell for leather down a single highway to reach each captured bridge in turn and help hold the ground while reinforcements were brought up. It would be a daring lightning strike that made use of the highly trained and motivated Airborne Army, and if successful offered tantalizing riches.

On the other hand, supply lines were so stretched that this operation would dominate Allied logistics, halt American drives to the south and would mean the task of clearing the long 30-mile River Scheldt that led to the vital Dutch port of Antwerp would have to be put on hold until it had run its course. And the only way it would succeed was if all the nine bridges were captured intact and the armoured thrust was able to get through to relieve the airborne troops holding them. It was high risk, to say the least.

Despite protests from General Omar Bradley, the US 2nd Army Group commander, and plenty of others besides, the Supreme Allied Commander, General Dwight D. Eisenhower, was persuaded Montgomery's plan was worth the attempt, partly for the chance of a route into Germany but also as a means of overrunning the V-2 rocket launch sites. Operation MARKET GARDEN was agreed on 10 September and launched just a week later on the 17th, by which time opposition had already stiffened considerably. One week was very little time to plan and execute such a complex operation – one that involved two American and one British airborne divisions, one Polish airborne brigade, the RAF and USAAF, and the British XXX Corps on the ground. There was no margin for error.

In the rush to get the operation ready, inevitably mistakes were made. At Arnhem itself, the British 1st Airborne Division was dropped too far from the bridge they had to capture, and because there were not enough aircraft to transport the entire airborne force in one go, half those landed had to remain at the landing zone to defend it before the next drop arrived. The bridge was captured by Major John Frost's 2nd Battalion, but there were not enough men there to hold it for long.

At Nimegen, the US 82nd Airborne focused on securing the Groesbeek Heights, the high ground at the edge of the German border, rather than going all-out to capture the giant bridge across the River Waal. The armoured thrust of XXX Corps struggled to keep the pace along the one road they had been allocated but reached Nijmegen on time, only to find the bridge had not yet been secured. By the time it was in Allied hands, the British paratroopers still holding Arnhem Bridge were too few in number and too short of ammunition to hold out against growing enemy reinforcements.

On 21 September, the Germans recaptured the bridge at Arnhem and although leading troops of XXX Corps were across the bridge at Nijmegen and less than ten miles away, they were too late to retake Arnhem and save the beleaguered paratroopers still holding out to the west of the town at Oosterbeek. On the night of 25 September, they withdrew back across the Rhine, MARKET GARDEN a failure. Although eight of the bridges had been captured intact, the one at Arnhem had proved a bridge too far.

Using the Airborne Army for a dramatic thrust was not in itself a bad idea, but the operation had been too complex with not enough time for preparation and planning. Its failure meant Eisenhower reverted to a broad-front strategy of applying pressure along much of the German border, though only limited operations could be carried out until the supply situation improved. In the northern half of the front, that meant clearing the Scheldt estuary leading to Antwerp, which was now heavily defended even though the deep-water port had been liberated on 3 September. Clearing the Scheldt was left to the Canadian Second Army and became a bitter slog through October. Crossing rivers, canals and dykes and moving through flat, flooded polder country was extremely difficult. Not until 8 November was the Scheldt finally cleared, after which the Germans had lost around 12,000 killed and wounded and 41,000 captured, and the Canadian Army some 12,900 casualties.

Meanwhile, the US First Army spent much of October fighting in and around the German border city of Aachen. 'Aachen was terrible,' said Tom Bowles, an infantryman of the 1st Division. 'Worse than Normandy.' The city finally fell to the Americans on the 21st, by which time Charlemagne's ancient capital was a shattered wreck.

Although by the autumn most of the Channel ports – Dunkirk excepted – were liberated by the Canadians, the destruction of French bridges and railways before D-Day now worked against the Allies in their drive east towards Germany. There were also civilian needs – shattered towns and villages and a lack of basic food – that worked against the installation of rapid supply lines.

Even so, by German standards, the Allies were still awash with men, materiel and supplies, but mindful of mounting casualties and the probable need to invade Japan once Germany was defeated, Eisenhower and his commanders did not want to send their infantry and tanks to be slaughtered. By pressing hard against the length of the German border, Eisenhower hoped to overwhelm the enemy defence, which was why, at the beginning of October, General Courtney Hodges found his US First Army being thrown into the dense Hürtgen Forest to the east of the Belgian city of Liège.

The original idea was to draw German troops away from the battle raging to the north at Aachen but also to capture the Rur Dam on the far side before the Germans blew it up and swamped the borderland downstream to the north. US commanders tended to opt for the straightest line to a target – and to the Rurstausee, that was straight through the Hürtgen Forest.

The forest was a terrible place through which to attack, however. Dense, craggy and with few roads to the west, it was also laced with bunkers, wire, mines and booby traps and every trail and track was overlooked by mortars, machine guns and gun positions. Allied air support was useless in such thick forest and the weather, terrible through the war-year winters, was closing in. The Hürtgen soon became a hellish battleground.

The initial attacks got nowhere but as October gave way to November, still more American units were flung into the meat grinder of the Hürtgen, which the Germans continued to reinforce through much easier lines of supply on their side of the border. A different option might have been to attack to the south-east of the forest, where the terrain was much easier, then cut up to the dam and bypass the Hürtgen entirely. But it wasn't to be.

To the south, General George S. Patton's Third Army crossed the River Moselle and attacked Metz in early November, a city he knew from his time there in the First World War, although the cut and dash of the summer was eroded by the rain, cold and mud and stiffening German defence. The city and most of its forts had fallen by 22 November. Even further south, the French and Americans of General Jake Devers's 12th Army Group also pressed eastwards. Casualties on both sides were high, but the Americans lost 118,698 casualties in November alone, and most of those were frontline troops.

With the Red Army in Bulgaria by early September, the Germans now struggled to extricate the 300,000 troops of Army Group E from Greece and the Western Balkans before Soviet forces trapped them there. With no naval strength and the Mediterranean closed to them, only streaming back overland would do.

Fortunately for Field Marshal Maximilian von Weichs, the Army Group E commander, the Red Army had its hands tied besieging Budapest in Hungary and so he was able to pull out his troops through Macedonia and Croatia even as Red Army troops were linking up with Tito's Yugoslavian partisans. The Soviet troops outraged Tito's Communists, however, by raping and pillaging the civilian population. This bought the Germans precious time.

Civil war, already simmering, now threatened to fully erupt throughout Greece. Determined that post-war Greece should not become a communist state and Soviet vassal, Churchill ordered British troops to be transferred from Italy to help disarm resistance groups and prevent a communist takeover. These were volatile, violent times, even away from the main battle fronts.

There was growing chaos within the Reich. Hitler's grip on power was as tight as ever, although he was by now a sick man, addled by a daily cocktail of drugs given by his doctor and increasingly paranoid about betrayal ever since the failed coup against the regime back in July. 'Honour' courts had been established to strip suspected officers of their titles. They would then be tried as civilians and invariably executed. Field Marshal Erwin Rommel, suspected of plotting against Hitler, was given the offer of suicide or public trial. On 14 October, he chose cyanide. Senior commanders were told to obey orders unconditionally and their families threatened if they failed to do so.

It was in this atmosphere of fear and paranoia that Hitler ordered a major German counter-thrust in the west. His plan was to smash through the Ardennes, the scene of his greatest triumph back in May 1940 and only lightly held by the Americans, and then drive a wedge between the British and Americans all the way to the key port of Antwerp. Incredibly, and in secret, the Germans managed to assemble a considerable force of two panzer armies without the Allies ever realizing what was going on. It was one of the reasons the Germans had fought so hard at the Hürtgen Forest: just behind it was one of the main assembly areas for Operation Wacht am Rhein – 'Watch on the Rhine'.

Snow lay thick on the ground in the hilly and wooded Ardennes that winter. In the early hours of 16 December, American troops, most recently arrived at the front and new to combat, were thinly holding the line when the skies opened and shells began screaming over. None of Hitler's generals thought the Führer's plan a good idea, as it had no realistic chance of success and every chance of depleting precious men, fuel and arms. But none dared show dissent.

And to begin with, the attack made progress. Speed was vital: they aimed to strike quickly and blaze a route to Antwerp before the Allies had a chance to offer any coordinated counter-attack. Two parallel offensives, the Sixth SS Panzer Army in the north and the Fifth Panzer Army in the south, burst through the American lines with a three-to-one manpower advantage and a two-to-one superiority in tanks and guns. Hitler had chosen December, when skies were leaden and the opportunities for the Allies to use their dominance in the air were fewer, but the falling snow made it harder for the attackers to stick to their strict timetable and slowed them down considerably.

Furthermore, the Americans in the area might have been green but they were not the French Army of 1940 and they quickly recovered their balance. As they fell back, they blew bridges, while determined stands were made at key crossroad towns like St Vith and at Bastogne, where the US 101st Airborne were hurriedly brought into the line. In the north, the rookie 99th Infantry Division held out on the Elsenborn Ridge, inflicting casualties on the Germans at a rate of eighteen to one, while behind them the 82nd Airborne helped halt Battlegroup Peiper, one of the main panzer thrusts. It was the actions of the 99th, above all, that were to prove decisive.

The German attack soon fell behind schedule. Capturing Allied fuel dumps had been a vital part of the plan, but the leading German units were unable to reach them; Battlegroup Peiper was forced to halt and then, on 23 December, pull back. Most of Peiper's tanks were abandoned as they ran out of fuel.

Overhead, the skies began to clear on the same day, and Allied aircraft thundered over in force, hammering German supply lines to the rear and shooting up troops on the roads. British forces were defending the River Meuse to the western edge of the Germans' furthest gains, while units from Patton's Third Army battled northwards to help relieve the situation around Bastogne. His troops reached the besieged town on Boxing Day, 26 December.

On the first day of 1945, the Luftwaffe, in a last-ditch effort, managed to launch Operation BODENPLATTE, a massed fighter attack of around 800 aircraft, which swept over the many Allied airfields now in Belgium and Holland. This attack caught the Allies by surprise, just as had the battle on the ground, and for the same reasons: because it was winter, because it made little tactical sense at this stage of the war, and because the Allies underestimated the Germans' ability to mount attacks on such scale. In all, around 300 Allied aircraft were destroyed, mostly on the ground, and over 150 damaged, but few pilots or aircrew were among the casualties and the aircraft losses were made good in around a week. In contrast, 143 Luftwaffe pilots were killed and 70 captured. Among the casualties were fourteen squadron commanders, an unrecoverable and devastating loss at this stage of the war. Rather like the attack on the ground, BODENPLATTE caused some short-term damage but in the longer term it was a terrible failure.

Officially, the Battle of the Bulge, as it became known, did not end until the third week of January, which was when almost all the Allied ground was recovered, but it had been lost to the Germans within a matter of days and BODENPLATTE was very much the last roll of the dice. There was, though, still one last German attack in the west to be played out.

Operation NORDWIND was launched far to the south in Alsace and Lorraine on 31 December and aimed to split the US Seventh and French First Armies, destroy them and seize back the city of Strasbourg. Like the Ardennes offensive, it was insanely overambitious. The Americans used the Maginot Line to help them defend the attack and although the fighting was bitter for several weeks, the Germans managed to stamp only a small salient, the Colmar Pocket, and on 25 January, the attack was called off.

By this time, they had even bigger battles to fight in the east. Hitler had been warned about the scale of the Soviet build-up along the Eastern Front but refused to believe the strengths of the Red Army now along the River Vistula. The Soviet way of war was to conduct massive offensives of comparatively short duration – around ten weeks – then pause for several months and pull back the battering ram for another swing. By 12 January, they were ready, with 4 million troops, nearly 10,000 tanks and some 40,000 guns and mortars.

Most German defences were swept aside. By 24 January, the Red Army had reached the Baltic, severing the historic city of Königsberg and East Prussia from the rest of the Reich. By the end of January, Red Army troops had reached the River Oder, 250 miles from their start point and less than 50 miles from Berlin.

As the Red Army swept through Poland, they liberated a number of extermination camps. Treblinka had been overrun the previous August, and Majdanek and Sobibor abandoned in the autumn, but the killing had continued at Chelmno and Auschwitz, which were finally liberated on 20 and 27 January. Around a million men, women and children, mostly Jews, had been murdered in the gas chambers at Auschwitz, and some 200,000 at Chelmno. The terrible depths of the Nazis' crimes were now laid bare.

The Germans were also starting to reap what they had sown with the vicious slaughter of Soviet troops and citizens during the years of occupation. Red Army troops now raped, murdered and pillaged tens of thousands of civilians as they swept into German territories. Many Germans preferred to take their own lives rather than succumb to the Russians. The orgy of violence in the east was set to continue.

Meanwhile, in February, President Roosevelt, Churchill and Stalin met at Yalta in the Crimea in southern Russia to discuss the post-war world. Britain was weary, its influence waning, and Roosevelt was in ill health, while Stalin was on home turf and in robust spirits; the outcome reflected the increased Soviet influence. By this time, the Americans especially were also increasingly concerned about the prospect of invading Japan in 1946 and anxious to preserve Allied lives and materiel in Europe as much as possible. At the end of the talks, among the points agreed was that Germany should be partitioned, east and west, Poland would be given new borders, shifting it west, and a communist government installed. Stalin agreed there should be democratic elections in Poland; he had no intention of sticking to this pledge, however. Yalta sowed the seeds of the future communist eastern bloc in Europe.

While the Red Army offensive halted in early February, on the Eastern Front, the Allies continued to push, amidst snow and freezing temperatures, through the Siegfried Line defences. While the Americans were busy pushing back the Bulge in the Ardennes, just to the north, the British XII Corps launched BLACKCOCK, an operation to push back the protruding Westwall around Heinsberg and to force the Germans back across the River Roer. It was part of a front-long attempt to straighten the line and close up further towards the River Rhine.

It is true that Allied armies had a longer logistical tail and fewer frontline troops than those in the Soviet or German Armies. In British Second Army, for example, 43 per cent were service troops while only 14 per cent were infantry and just 8 per cent were armoured units. However, for those in the infantry or in tanks, whether British, American or Canadian, the chances of getting through the fighting unscathed were statistically zero, as they were for German, Soviet and any other frontline troops. And whether one was lightly wounded, badly wounded or killed was really a matter of chance.

The conditions in the winter of 1944/45 were also terrible. In October and November, it rained almost endlessly, so that wherever fighting took place they were soon battling through quagmires of mud. Then, at the beginning of December, temperatures dropped and a blanket of snow fell across much of northern Europe. Life at the front line was relentless – there was none of the regular rotation of troops every few days as there had been on the Western Front in the First World War. Rather, troops could find themselves living in a foxhole in the ground, surrounded by mud or snow, for long weeks at a time. Everyone suffered. It was brutal.

The major Allied offensive for February 1945 focused on Montgomery's 21st Army Group part of the front to the north. Operation VERITABLE was to be led by the Canadian First Army, but with British XXX Corps attached. Also under Montgomery's command was the US Ninth Army, led by the very capable General William Simpson. The plan was for a two-fisted punch, with the Canadians with XXX Corps to strike first through the Reichswald, the mighty forest on the German border between Nijmegen and Cleve, then a little later, Simpson's Ninth Army would strike across the River Roer and link up with the British and Canadians. Together, they would then move up to the Rhine, clearing the Rhineland to the west. Then, in March, once the weather had started to improve, all along the front there would be a drive to cross the mighty river and make strides into the heart of the Reich.

VERITABLE began on 9 February, following the bombing of the medieval city of Cleve and the neighbouring town of Goch by the Allied heavies. This achieved very little except to destroy two historic towns, offer rubble defences for the defenders and block a huge number of roads, which needed to be cleared before the ground troops could push on through. For the most part, the Allied armies were, by this stage of the war, well equipped, well trained and well led, but despite the early lessons of Monte Cassino, Caen and St Lô, all of which were similarly pulverized with no appreciable benefit to the attackers, General Brian Horrocks, the XXX Corps commander, still ordered Goch and Cleve to be flattened before launching his attack.

To make matters worse, the Germans smashed the Rhine's dykes and so flooded the northern part of the battlefield as soon as the offensive had begun. The Allies faced two enemies: the Germans and the conditions.

None the less, by using amphibious DUKWs and other such vehicles, the British and Canadians were able to maintain their advance. The Reichswald was cleared, as were Cleve and Goch, and the forward units continued to push south-east and east towards the Rhine.

To the south, Simpson's Ninth Army was also lined up to cross the River Roer in what was intended to be the second part of the two-fisted punch. Unfortunately, the Roer was now also flooded, because although First Army had finally got through the Hürtgen and reached the dams further south, the retreating Germans had destroyed the spillways and control machinery, so that a torrent had gushed downriver towards Ninth Army. Only on 21 February, with the floodwaters finally receding, was Simpson able to finally launch Operation GRENADE.

Despite the conditions, the combined attacks of VERITABLE and GRENADE hammered the German Fifteenth and First Parachute Armies. Field Marshal Walter Model, the German Army Group commander, pleaded with Hitler to withdraw back across the Rhine. Hitler refused permission.

On the Eastern Front, meanwhile, the Germans had counter-attacked in Pomerania, briefly gaining some ground, before Marshals Zhukov and Rokossovsky went on the offensive again, blasting their way across West Prussia and Pomerania until their armies were all lined up along the Oder. To the south, the Germans were still furiously defending Budapest, although increasingly desperately and hopelessly.

The Reich was imploding, however. In February, the Reichsbahn, the German railway, which had been the glue that kept the German war effort going, finally collapsed. Armageddon was approaching.

It was already upon many of those Germans stranded in the besieged city of Königsberg and the rest of East Prussia. A massive seaborne evacuation was launched in January and by the war's end an incredible 2 million had been rescued by the Kriegsmarine, the German navy, many in vessels barely fit to go to sea. Plenty did not make it, however, including some 9,500 crammed into the battered Baltic liner *Wilhelm Gustloff* when it was sunk by a Soviet submarine. It remains the largest number of lives lost on a single ship.

While the Red Army paused for breath along the Oder ahead of its final assault towards Berlin, the Allies were, by March, getting ready to cross the Rhine. All the bridges over the river were blown by the retreating Germans – except one, a railway bridge at the small town of Remagen. On 7 March, leading elements of the 9th Armored Division of the US First Army, using the newly arrived bigger Pershing tanks, neared the bridge. Suddenly, first one, then two explosions erupted as German engineers detonated charges to drop the bridge into the river below. To the amazement of American and German alike, however, when the smoke cleared, the bridge was still standing. Incredibly, the charges had lifted it up into the air only for it to land back down on its pillars.

Without waiting for orders, infantrymen, with covering fire from the Pershings, ran across it, driving the Germans back. By nightfall, tanks were across the river and within 24 hours the Americans had 8,000 men across. It was a bridgehead they were able to hold as more men, then divisions, crossed the bridge at Remagen.

Hitler's commanders had urged him to allow his beleaguered forces to fall back behind the huge barrier of the Rhine far earlier, but he had insisted they fight to the west of the river to the last man. As a result, around 300,000 men were killed, wounded or captured.

This meant there were fewer German forces to face the Allies on the eastern side of the Rhine. American generals have been criticized for not rapidly pushing beyond the Rhine at Remagen, but Eisenhower and Bradley wanted to continue with the strategy of piling immense pressure on the remaining German forces along a broad front. Germany might be imploding but there were still many prepared to fanatically fight on and the prospect of an invasion of Japan – one that was expected to cost millions in casualties – loomed large. It was neither productive nor necessary to throw caution to the wind at this stage.

Rhine crossings were meticulously planned to the north and south in the third week of May and all were successful. Montgomery's crossing at Rees and Wesel was additionally supported by the most effective airborne drop of the war and huge artillery bombardment, as there were very good reasons for the exhausted British, now worryingly short of frontline manpower, not to take any chances either.

Even after the crossings, there were still a few stings in the Germans' tail – one US armoured column was destroyed as it tried to overrun an SS panzer training centre near Paderborn. Even so, Simpson's Ninth Army to the north and Hodges' First to the south swiftly encircled the Ruhr industrial heartland, capturing a further 317,000 enemy troops. It was clear the end of the war was near.

While the Allies crossed the Rhine, the Red Army continued its build-up for the latest swing of the battering ram. Three fronts – what the Soviets termed groups of armies – were now lined up along the Oder. In the north was Rokossovsky's 2nd Belorussian Front, directly east of Berlin was Georgy Zhukov's 1st Belorussian Front and to the south of Zhukov was Marshal Ivan Konev's 1st Ukrainian Front: in all, 2.4 million men, 41,600 guns, 6,250 tanks and 7,500 aircraft. Against them were some 750,000 troops, which included two understrength army groups. Not one division was full strength, and many units were made up of teenage boys and older men earlier excused duty due to their age. The German situation was desperate, to say the least.

Stalin deliberately egged on Zhukov and Konev to race against one another to the heart of Berlin. Zhukov, although closer, had to deal with the Oder crossings and the natural defences of the Seelow Heights, 35 miles west of Berlin, and although, when the storm broke on 14 April, his forces were so overwhelming they could hardly fail, it took him five days and horrific numbers of casualties to smash this first line of defence. German trenches on the Seelow Heights can still be seen to this day.

Further south, Vienna, the Austrian capital, was taken by the Red Army on 13 April, while over Berlin itself, RAF Bomber Command continued to pound the city by night. By the last raid, on 18/19 April, the Nazi capital was a wreck, a once great city reduced to rubble, its surviving citizens scavenging to survive in the cellars below. The following day, 20 April, was Hitler's birthday. From his bunker in the heart of Berlin, his twelve-year rule was now very near the end.

In the west, the Allies continued to find a mixture of willing surrender and fanatical resistance, although Patton's Third Army, especially, now hurtled eastwards into Bavaria and then Austria, capturing Linz, Hitler's home town. Prague was Third Army's for the taking, but he was ordered to leave the Czechoslovakian capital for the Soviets.

It was now the Western Allies' turn to discover the horrific depths of the Nazis' warped ideology. Third Army overran slave labour camps around the V-2 rocket production site at Ohrdruf and at Nordhausen. 'Rows upon rows of skin-coloured skeletons,' wrote Charles MacDonald, an American veteran. 'One girl in particular I noticed; I would say she was about seventeen years old. She lay as she had fallen, gangrened and naked.' On 15 April, British troops liberated Belsen, a concentration rather than a death camp, but where overcrowding and inhuman treatment had led to catastrophic numbers of dead and dying. 'The living lay with their heads against the corpses and around them moved the awful, ghostly procession of emaciated, aimless people, with nothing and with no hope of life,' wrote the journalist Richard Dimbleby. 'This day at Belsen was the most horrible of my life.' There were plenty more camps besides, each with their share of tragedy, misery and suffering.

The fighting continued. Montgomery's forces were hurrying towards the Baltic. At any moment, though, German troops would pounce with *Panzerfausts*, short-range propelled charges, destroying another tank or vehicle. The end was so close, but it was still not over.

On 20 April, Rokossovsky launched his attack north of the city and up to the Baltic Coast. That same day, Zossen, to the south-east of Berlin and the German Army's underground bunker headquarters, was captured by Konev's men.

On 25 April, while the battle still raged in Berlin, Red Army troops from a guards rifle regiment in Konev's 1st Ukrainian Front met with Americans of the 69th Division, part of First Army, on the River Elbe at Torgau. A little way to the north, Simpson's Ninth Army swept through Hanover and then captured Brunswick and Magdeburg, three cities also ravaged by repeated Allied bombing. Simpson was all for pushing on to Potsdam and then Berlin, but he was ordered to hold where he was and leave it to the Soviets.

Eisenhower's decision not to fight all the way to Berlin certainly saved Allied lives. In contrast, Zhukov and Konev's forces were experiencing brutal casualty rates despite their overwhelming strength. To a certain extent, this was because Zhukov, especially, was pushing his men particularly hard in his efforts to win Berlin, but it was also because the Germans, depleted and beaten though they were, still fought on.

In his bunker beneath the Reichs Chancellory, Hitler had refused to flee as his inner circle had urged him to do. Rather, he had accepted his life would end there, in Berlin, with the final collapse of the Third Reich. It did not stop him from ranting at his generals' failings, however, or demanding yet more counter-attacks that could not possibly be mounted. Much of Berlin had been overrun by 30 April, the day on which he decided to take his life, shooting himself in the temple at around 3.20 p.m. Afterwards, his body, and that of his wife of one day, Eva Braun, were burned just outside the bunker entrance. Later that day, the Soviet flag was raised above the Reichstag, the German parliament building, no more than a mile from the bunker.

German forces surrendered in Italy on 2 May, the same day that General Helmuth Weidling raised the white flag in Berlin. At 8 a.m. on the 5th, all German forces in Northern Germany and Denmark surrendered to Montgomery's 21st Army Group. Elsewhere, the fighting continued as Grand Admiral Karl Dönitz, who had taken over as Führer on Hitler's death, frantically tried to get as many troops – and civilians – into Western Allied-held territory as possible. The evacuation of Danzig and East Prussia also continued until the end, by which time a staggering 2 million people had escaped.

Finally, at 2.41 a.m. on 7 May, a German delegation led by General Alfred Jodl surrendered to Eisenhower at Supreme Headquarters in Reims in France. The Allies had demanded unconditional surrender – that is, no German terms at all – and had got it. The Soviet Union, however, wanted their own surrender ceremony and would not allow the announcement of the end of the war until theirs had been completed in Berlin.

It was a farcical situation, and inevitably the news got out, although via a German rather than Allied leak. The British and Americans declared 8 May to be VE Day – Victory in Europe Day. Celebrations were held around the free world – from London to Paris to Sydney and Toronto as millions cheered, drank and partied.

The Soviet surrender ceremony was finally conducted in an old barracks at Karlshorst in south-east Berlin, in the very first minutes of 9 May. As President Truman and Prime Minister Winston Churchill were both aware, however, and made clear in their victory speeches, the war was not over yet. There was still Imperial Japan to crush too. But the war in Europe was finally at an end and the Nazis, and all they stood for, crushed. A new, and very different, Europe would emerge from the ruins.